Georgia, My State
Geographic Regions

Valley and Ridge

by Doraine Bennett

STATE STANDARDS PUBLISHING

Your State • Your Standards • Your Grade Level

Dear Educators, Librarians and Parents . . .

Thank you for choosing the *"Georgia, My State"* Series! We have designed this series to support the Georgia Department of Education's Georgia Performance Standards for elementary level Georgia studies. Each book in the series has been written at appropriate grade level as measured by the ATOS Readability Formula for Books (Accelerated Reader), the Lexile Framework for Reading, and the Fountas & Pinnell Benchmark Assessment System for Guided Reading. Photographs and/or illustrations, captions, and other design elements have been included to provide supportive visual messaging to enhance text comprehension. Glossary and Word Index sections introduce key new words and help young readers develop skills in locating and combining information.

We wish you all success in using the *"Georgia, My State"* Series to meet your student or child's learning needs. For additional sources of information, see www.georgiaencyclopedia.org.

Jill Ward, President

Publisher
State Standards Publishing, LLC
1788 Quail Hollow
Hamilton, GA 31811
USA
1.866.740.3056
www.statestandardspublishing.com

Library of Congress Cataloging-in-Publication Data
Bennett, Doraine, 1953-
  Valley and Ridge / by Doraine Bennett.
      p. cm. -- (Georgia, my state. Geographic Regions)
  Includes index.
  ISBN-13: 978-1-935077-23-7 (hardcover)
  ISBN-10: 1-935077-23-6 (hardcover)
  ISBN-13: 978-1-935077-28-2 (pbk.)
  ISBN-10: 1-935077-28-7 (pbk.)
  1. Georgia--Juvenile literature. 2. Georgia--Geography--Juvenile literature. I. Title.
  F286.3.B468 2009
  917.58'3--dc22
                                    2009013006

Table of Contents

The Valley and Ridge region looks like this.

Appalachian Plateau

Blue Ridge

Valley and Ridge

Piedmont

Upper Coastal Plain

Lower Coastal Plain

MY STATE

It is in the northwest part of Georgia.

Let's Explore!

Hi, I'm Bagster! Let's explore the Valley and Ridge **geographic region**. A region is an area named for the way the land is formed. The Valley and Ridge is between the **Blue Ridge Mountains** and the **Appalachian Plateau**. Can you find it on a map? It's in the northwest part of Georgia.

Ridge

Valley

Valley

What is a Ridge?
What is a Valley?

The roof of a house has two sides. The sides slope upward. They meet and form a line called a **ridge**. Small mountains in the Valley and Ridge slope upward. They meet each other in a ridge. The low land beside them is called a **valley**.

The Armuchee Ridges rise up from the valleys.

Tennessee

Chickamauga Valley

Armuchee Ridges

Great Valley

Alabama

Valley
and
Ridge
Region

The valleys run side by side like railroad tracks.

Can You Name the Valleys and Ridges?

The Valley and Ridge has three main parts. The **Chickamauga Valley** is here. The **Great Valley** is here. The **Armuchee Ridges** are here. The valleys are long and straight. They run side by side like railroad tracks. The Armuchee Ridges rise up between the valleys.

The valleys go from Alabama to Tennessee.

Tennessee

Chickamauga Valley
Armuchee Ridges
Great Valley

Alabama

Traveling is easier in the valley.

Which Direction Should We Go?

Let's start in the southwest part of the region. It is near Alabama. We can go northeast through the valleys. We can go to Tennessee. Many Indians, soldiers, and animals have gone this way before us. The valleys made traveling easier.

The Indians grew corn, beans, and squash in the good soil.

Indians in the Valley and Ridge buried their chiefs in mounds like this.

What are Those Mounds?

The first Indians in the Valley and Ridge were **mound builders**. They buried their chiefs in the **Etowah Mounds**. Chiefs built their homes on the mounds. They built cities in the valleys. They grew corn, beans, and squash in the good soil.

Sequoyah brought his Cherokee alphabet to New Echota.

The Cherokee newspaper was printed here.

Sequoyah Was Here!

Sequoyah came to **New Echota**. It is in the Great Valley. Sequoyah was a Cherokee Indian. He invented the Cherokee alphabet. He showed his alphabet to the Cherokee leaders here. The Cherokee newspaper was printed here.

Forests cover the Armuchee ridges

We can paddle a canoe in the national forest.

What is a National Forest?

Forests cover the Armuchee Ridges. The forests are part of the **Chattahoochee National Forest**. A national forest is a place where land is protected. People cannot build things there without permission. But we can paddle a canoe in the national forest!

Rocks

Fault

Land sometimes slips at a fault. Rocks push up out of the ground.

What is a Fault?

Rocks in the Blue Ridge Mountains rest against rocks in the Great Valley. These rocks meet at the **Cartersville-Great Smoky Fault**. A **fault** is a deep crack inside the earth. Sometimes the land slips at a fault. Rocks push up out of the ground.

There are fossils of coral in the Valley and Ridge.
Coral lives in the ocean!

Coral Fossils

Living Coral

This leaf was trapped in the rocks. It made a fossil.

What Lived Here Long Ago?

Fossils are the remains of dead plants or animals. They lived long ago. Their remains were trapped in rocks. Fossils can be footprints or teeth or bones. They can be leaf shapes pressed into the rock. There are lots of fossils in the Valley and Ridge! Let's look for fossils!

Glossary

Appalachian Plateau – The geographic region to the west of the Valley and Ridge.

Armuchee Ridges – Small mountains in the Valley and Ridge.

Blue Ridge Mountains – The geographic region to the east of the Valley and Ridge.

Cartersville-Great Smoky Fault – A deep crack inside the earth of the Valley and Ridge.

Chattahoochee National Forest – The forest that covers the Armuchee Ridges.

Chickamauga Valley – The low, flat land to the west of the Armuchee Ridges.

Etowah Mounds – An Indian burial ground and village site in the Valley and Ridge.

fault – A deep crack inside the earth.

fossils – The remains of dead plants and animals that lived long ago.

geographic region – An area named for the way the land is formed.

Great Valley – The low, flat land to the east of the Armuchee Ridges.

mound builders – Native American tribes who made large hills of earth to bury their chiefs in, or put buildings on.

New Echota – The place where the first Cherokee newspaper was printed.

ridge – The place where two sloped sides meet.

valley – The low land beside a mountain or ridge.

Word Index

Image Credits

About the Author

Doraine Bennett has a degree in professional writing from Columbus State University in Columbus, Georgia, and has been writing and teaching writing for over twenty years. She has authored numerous articles in magazines for both children and adults and is the editor of the National Infantry Association's *Infantry Bugler* magazine. Doraine enjoys reading and writing books and articles for children. She lives in Georgia with her husband, Cliff.